W9-ACK-241

RESCUED! ANIMAL ESCAPES

Wildfire Escape

PET ANIMALS RESCUE!

By James Buckley Jr.

Illustrated by Kerstin LaCross

BEARPORT
PUBLISHING

Minneapolis, Minnesota

BEAR CLAW

Credits

Interior coloring by Jon Siruno.
Interior inks by Haley Boros.

Photos: 22T © Chris Carlson/AP Photo; 22B © AP Photo.

Bearport Publishing
Minneapolis, MN
President: Jen Jenson
Director of Product Development: Spencer Brinker
Editor: Allison Juda

Produced by Shoreline Publishing Group LLC
Santa Barbara, California
Designer: Patty Kelley
Editorial Director: James Buckley Jr.

DISCLAIMER: This graphic story is a dramatization based on true events. It is intended to give the reader a sense of the narrative rather than a presentation of actual details as they occurred.

Library of Congress Cataloging-in-Publication Data

Names: Buckley, James, Jr., 1963- author. | LaCross, Kerstin, 1988-
    illustrator.
Title: Wildfire escape : pet animals rescue! / by James Buckley Jr. ;
    illustrated by Kerstin LaCross.
Description: Bear claw books edition. | Minneapolis, Minnesota : Bearport
    Publishing Company, [2021] | Series: Rescued! animal escapes | Includes
    bibliographical references and index.
Identifiers: LCCN 2020039095 (print) | LCCN 2020039096 (ebook) | ISBN
    9781647476229 (library binding) | ISBN 9781647476298 (paperback) | ISBN
    9781647476366 (ebook)
Subjects: LCSH: Wildfires—California—Juvenile literature. | Animal
    rescue—California—Juvenile literature. | Pets—Juvenile literature.
Classification: LCC SD421.32.C2 B83 2021 (print) | LCC SD421.32.C2
    (ebook) | DDC 363.37/909794—dc23
LC record available at https://lccn.loc.gov/2020039095
LC ebook record available at https://lccn.loc.gov/2020039096

For more information, write to Bearport Publishing, 5357 Penn Avenue South, Minneapolis, MN 55419. Printed in the United States of America.

CONTENTS

CHAPTER 1

Wildfire!

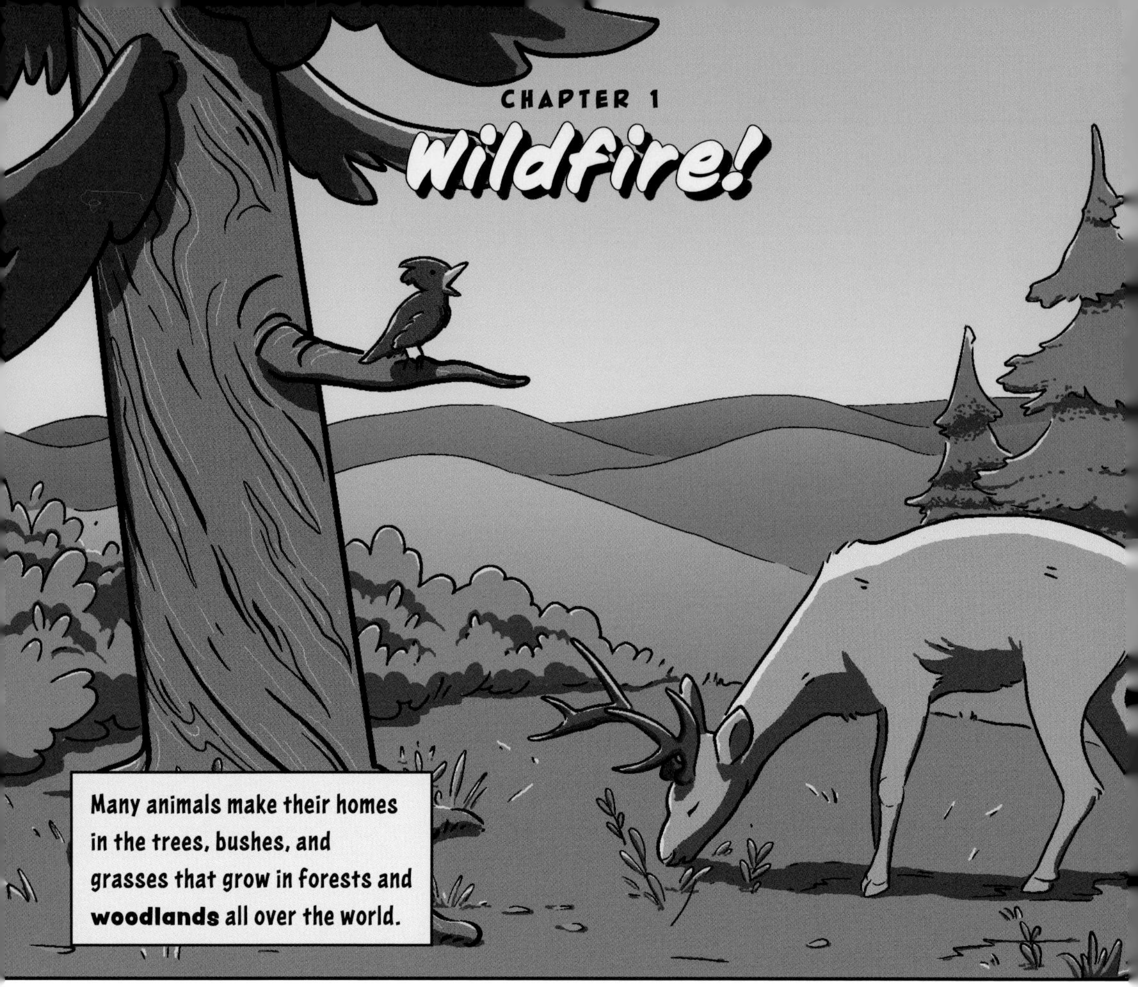
Many animals make their homes in the trees, bushes, and grasses that grow in forests and **woodlands** all over the world.

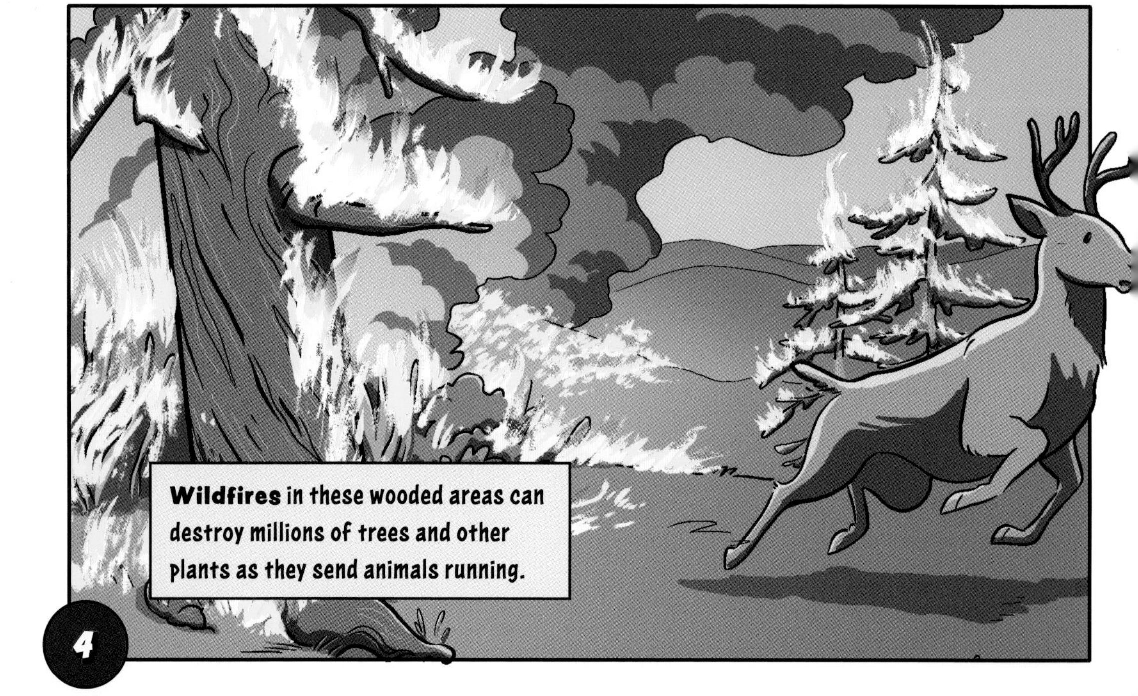
Wildfires in these wooded areas can destroy millions of trees and other plants as they send animals running.

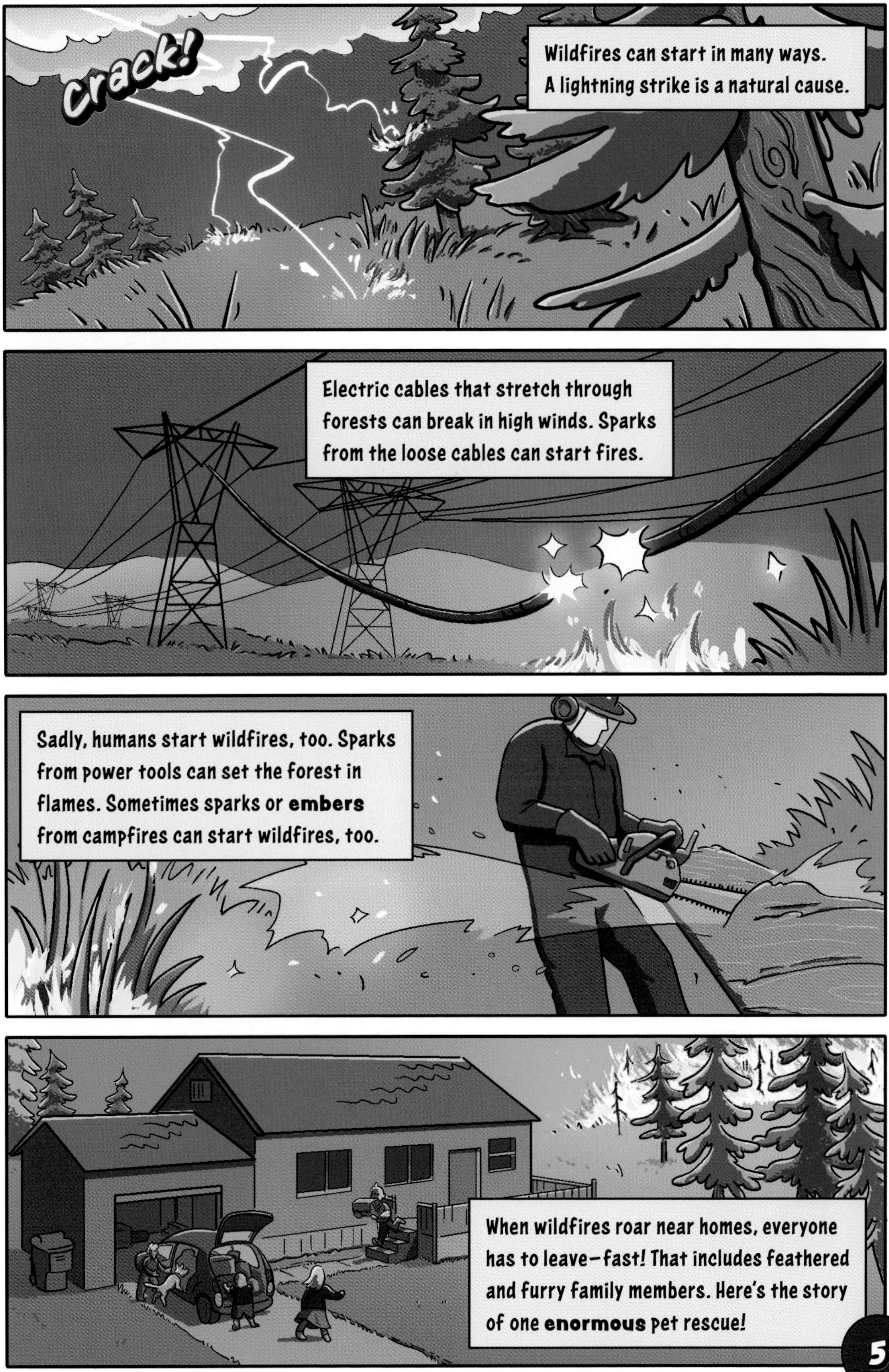
Crack!
Wildfires can start in many ways. A lightning strike is a natural cause.
Electric cables that stretch through forests can break in high winds. Sparks from the loose cables can start fires.
Sadly, humans start wildfires, too. Sparks from power tools can set the forest in flames. Sometimes sparks or **embers** from campfires can start wildfires, too.
When wildfires roar near homes, everyone has to leave—fast! That includes feathered and furry family members. Here's the story of one **enormous** pet rescue!

CHAPTER 2

A Careless Camper

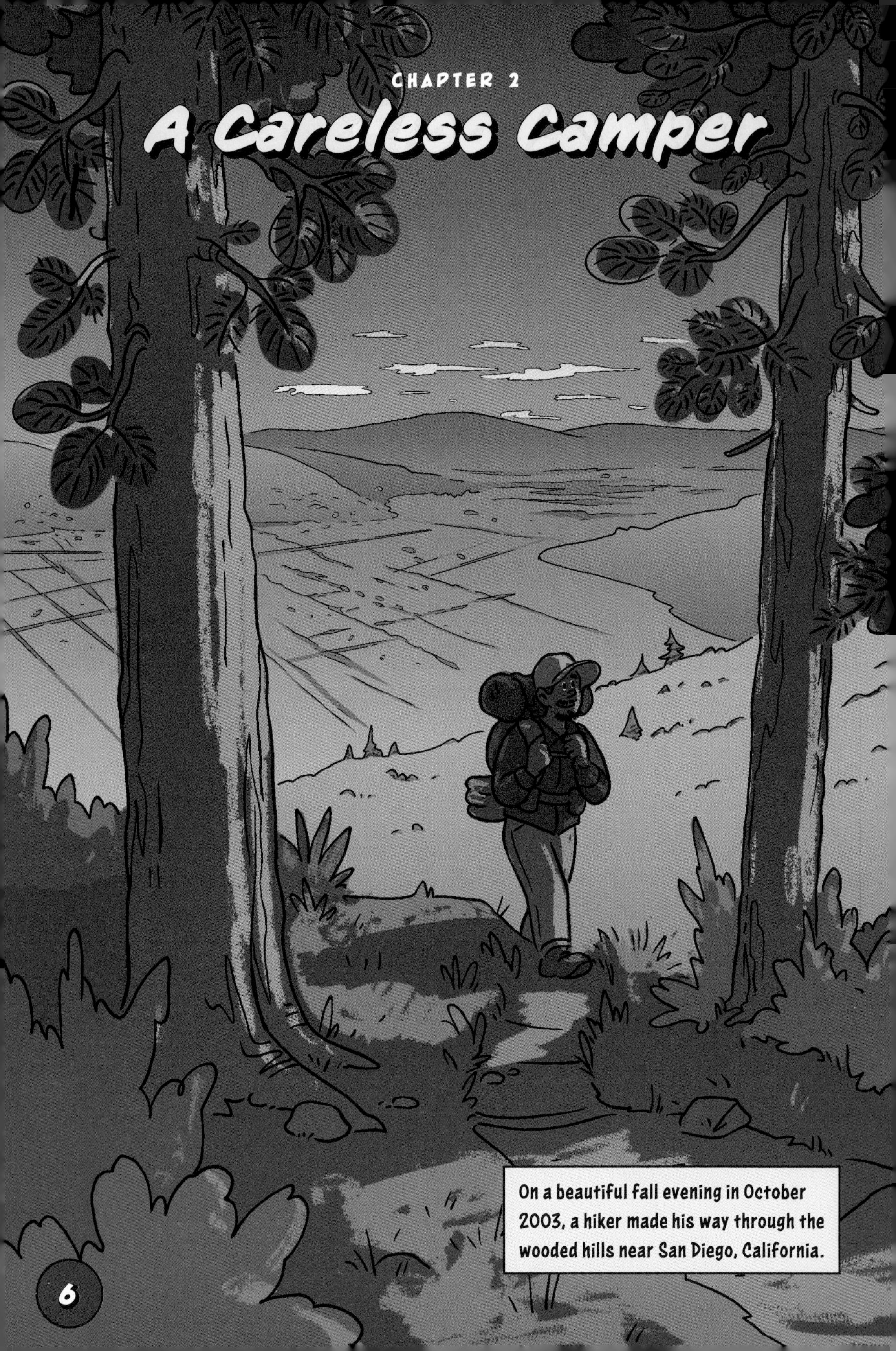
On a beautiful fall evening in October 2003, a hiker made his way through the wooded hills near San Diego, California.

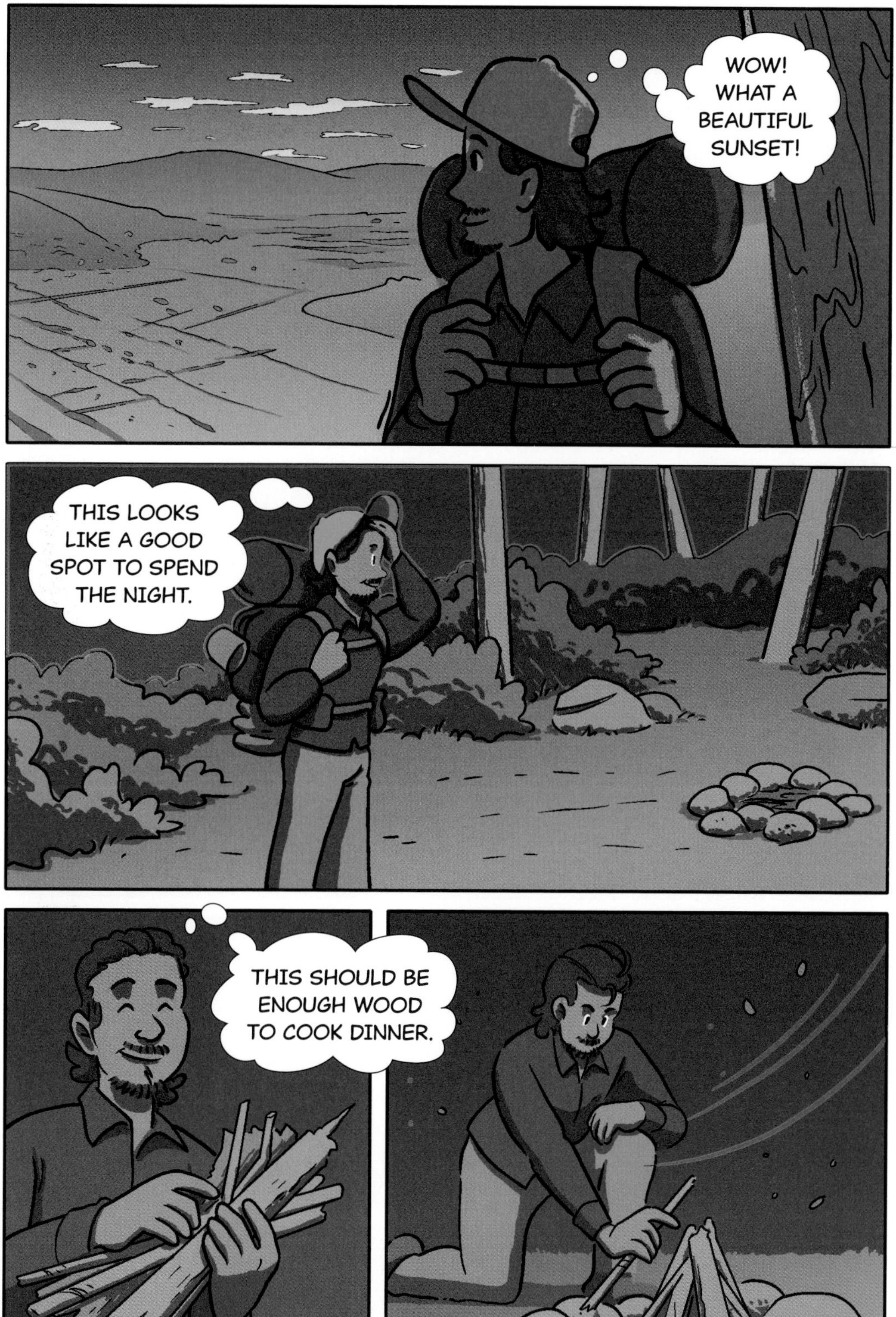
WOW! WHAT A BEAUTIFUL SUNSET!
THIS LOOKS LIKE A GOOD SPOT TO SPEND THE NIGHT.
THIS SHOULD BE ENOUGH WOOD TO COOK DINNER.

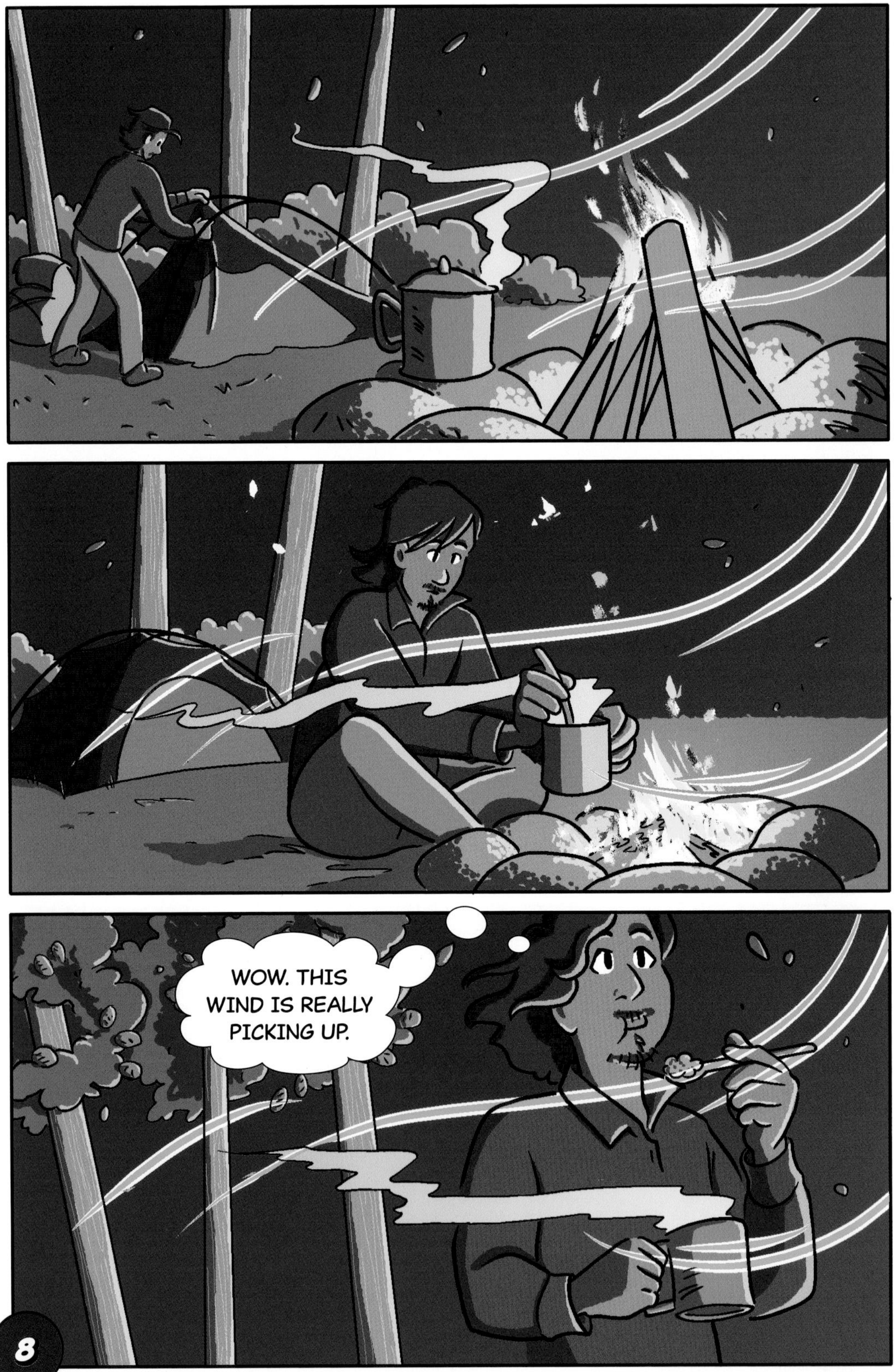
WOW. THIS WIND IS REALLY PICKING UP.

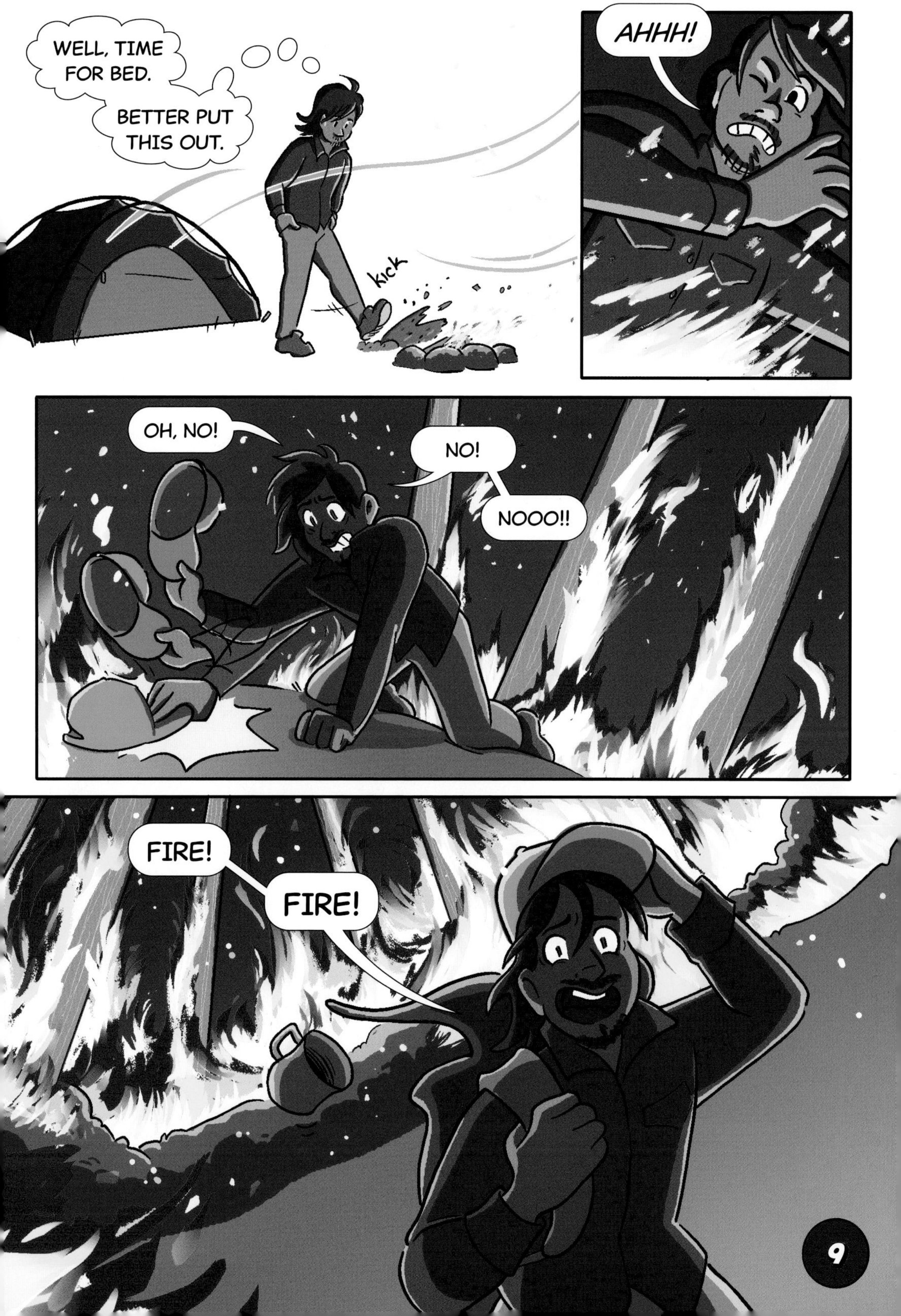
WELL, TIME FOR BED.
BETTER PUT THIS OUT.
kick
AHHH!
OH, NO!
NO!
NOOO!!
FIRE!
FIRE!

CHAPTER 3

Animals in Danger

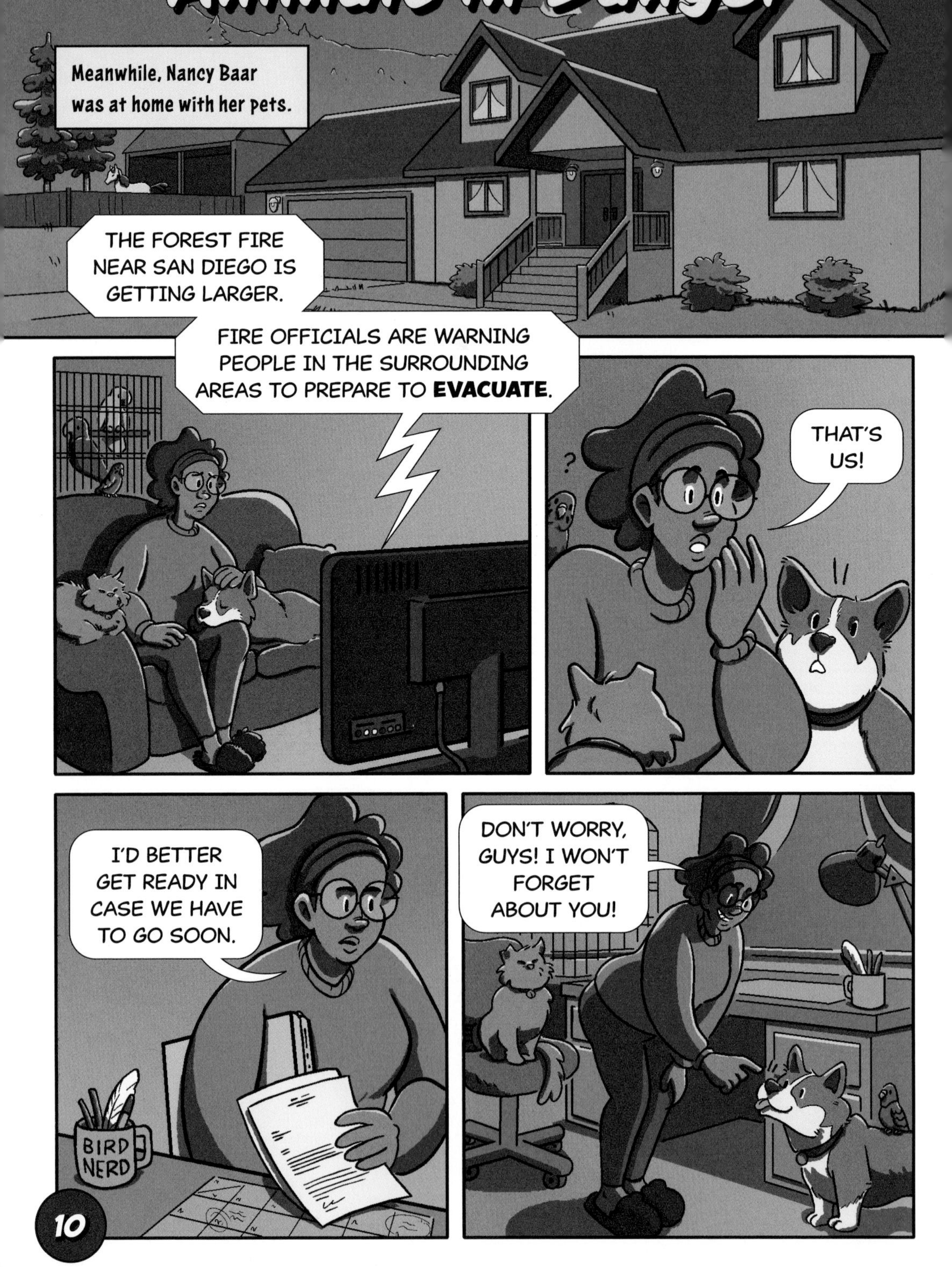

Meanwhile, Nancy Baar was at home with her pets.
THE FOREST FIRE NEAR SAN DIEGO IS GETTING LARGER.
FIRE OFFICIALS ARE WARNING PEOPLE IN THE SURROUNDING AREAS TO PREPARE TO **EVACUATE**.
?
THAT'S US!
I'D BETTER GET READY IN CASE WE HAVE TO GO SOON.
BIRD NERD
DON'T WORRY, GUYS! I WON'T FORGET ABOUT YOU!

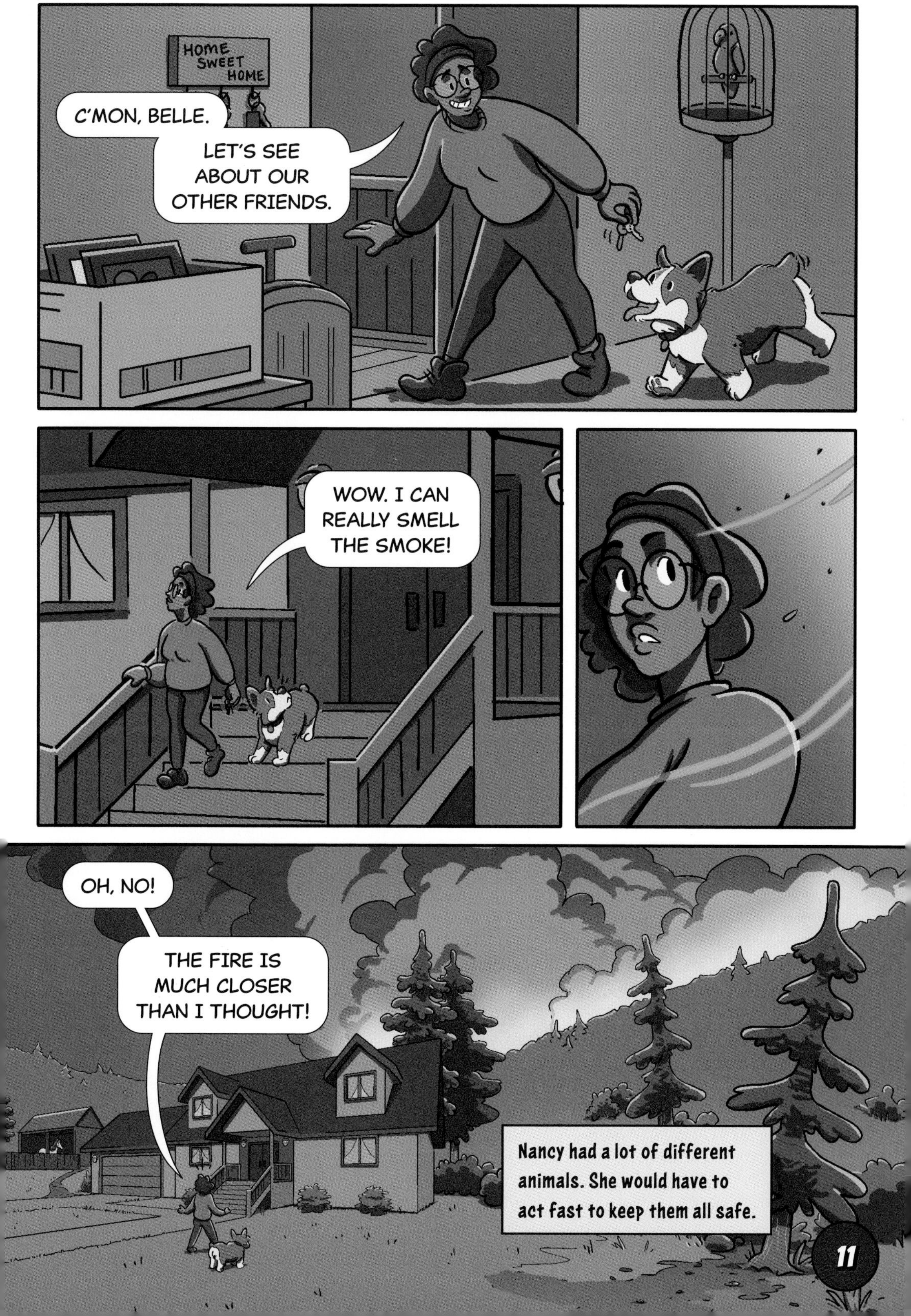
HOME SWEET HOME
C'MON, BELLE.
LET'S SEE ABOUT OUR OTHER FRIENDS.
WOW. I CAN REALLY SMELL THE SMOKE!
OH, NO!
THE FIRE IS MUCH CLOSER THAN I THOUGHT!
Nancy had a lot of different animals. She would have to act fast to keep them all safe.

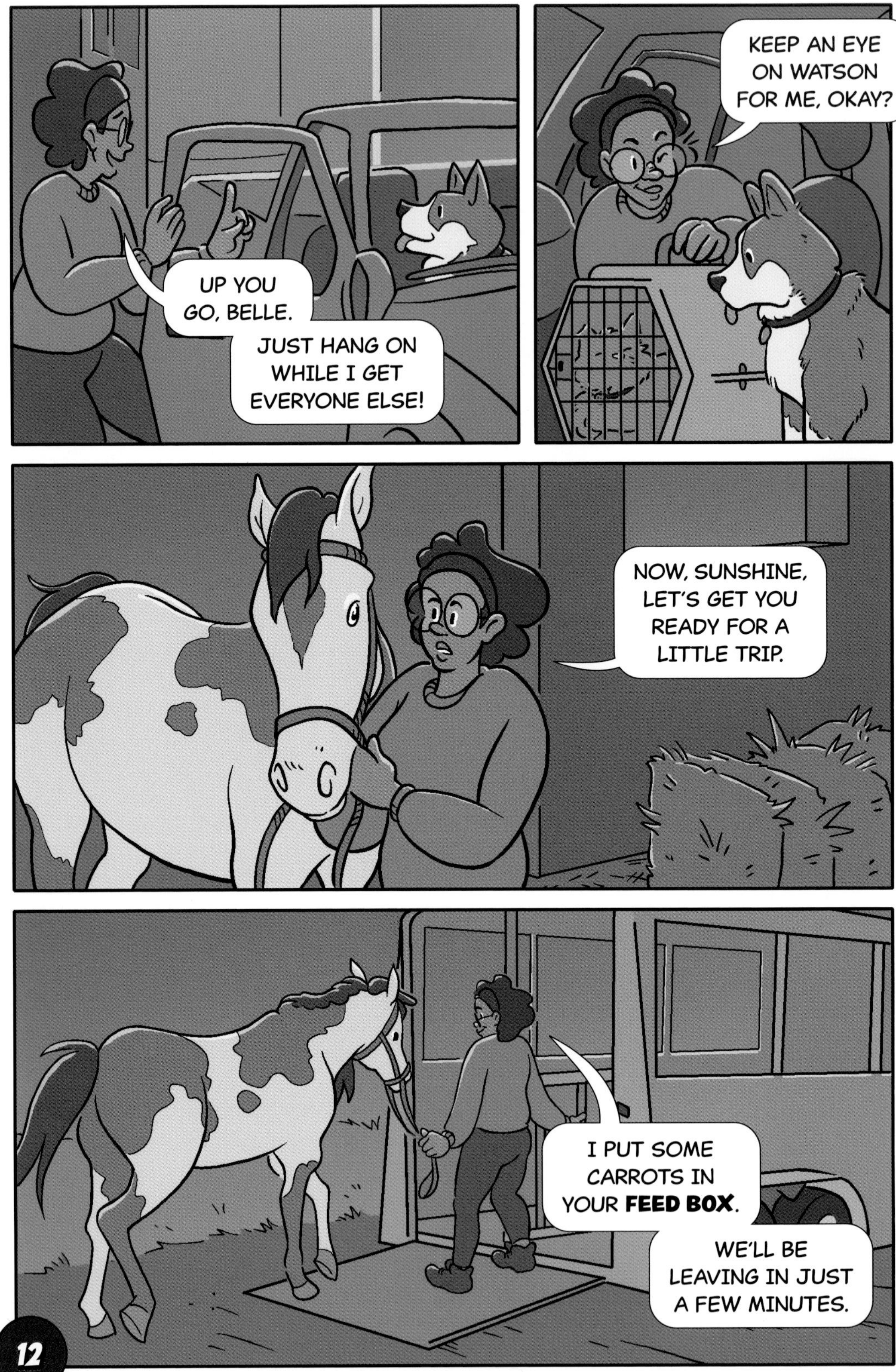
UP YOU GO, BELLE.
JUST HANG ON WHILE I GET EVERYONE ELSE!
KEEP AN EYE ON WATSON FOR ME, OKAY?
NOW, SUNSHINE, LET'S GET YOU READY FOR A LITTLE TRIP.
I PUT SOME CARROTS IN YOUR **FEED BOX**.
WE'LL BE LEAVING IN JUST A FEW MINUTES.

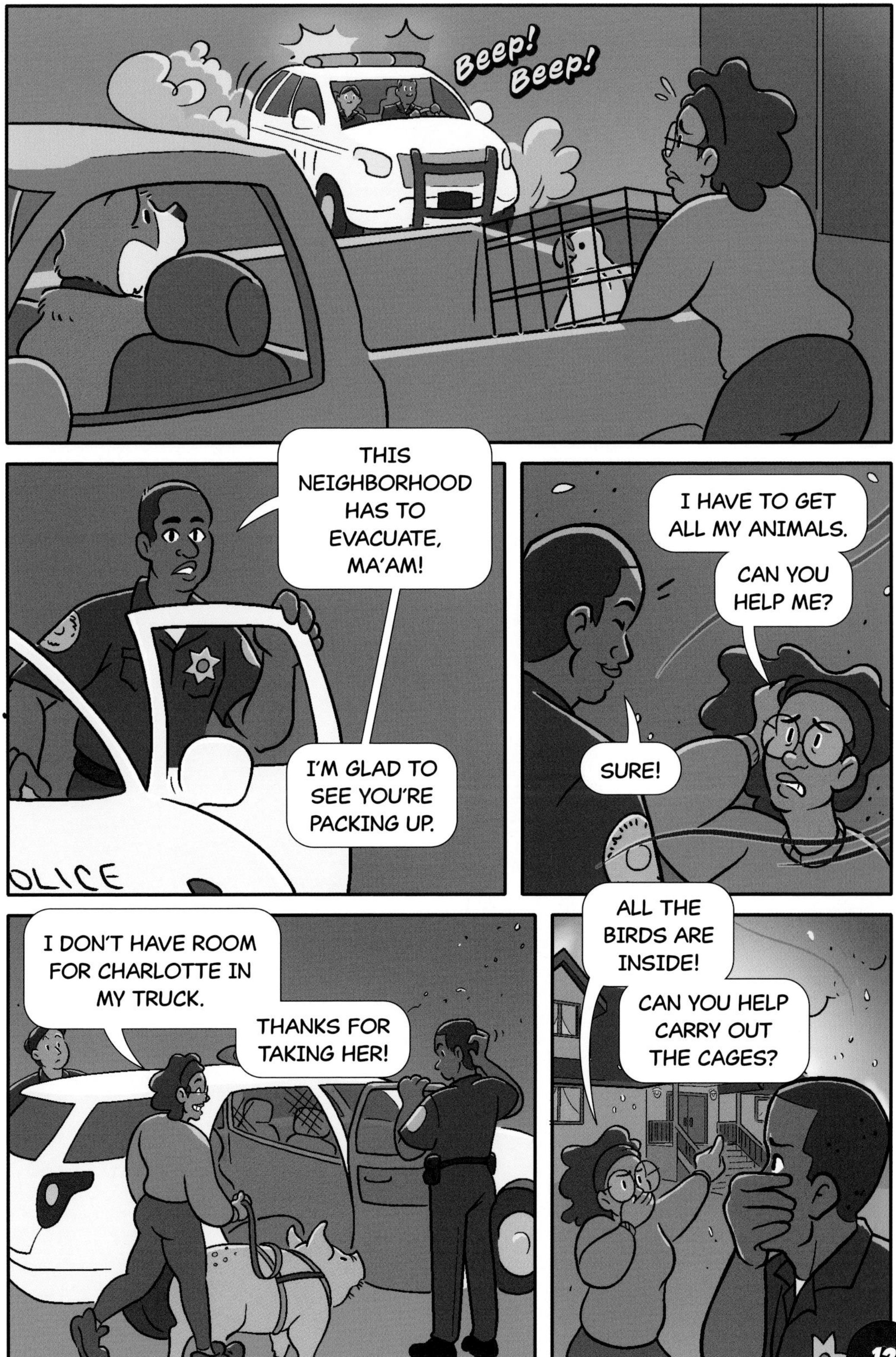
Beep! Beep!
THIS NEIGHBORHOOD HAS TO EVACUATE, MA'AM!
I'M GLAD TO SEE YOU'RE PACKING UP.
I HAVE TO GET ALL MY ANIMALS.
CAN YOU HELP ME?
SURE!
I DON'T HAVE ROOM FOR CHARLOTTE IN MY TRUCK.
THANKS FOR TAKING HER!
ALL THE BIRDS ARE INSIDE!
CAN YOU HELP CARRY OUT THE CAGES?
OLICE

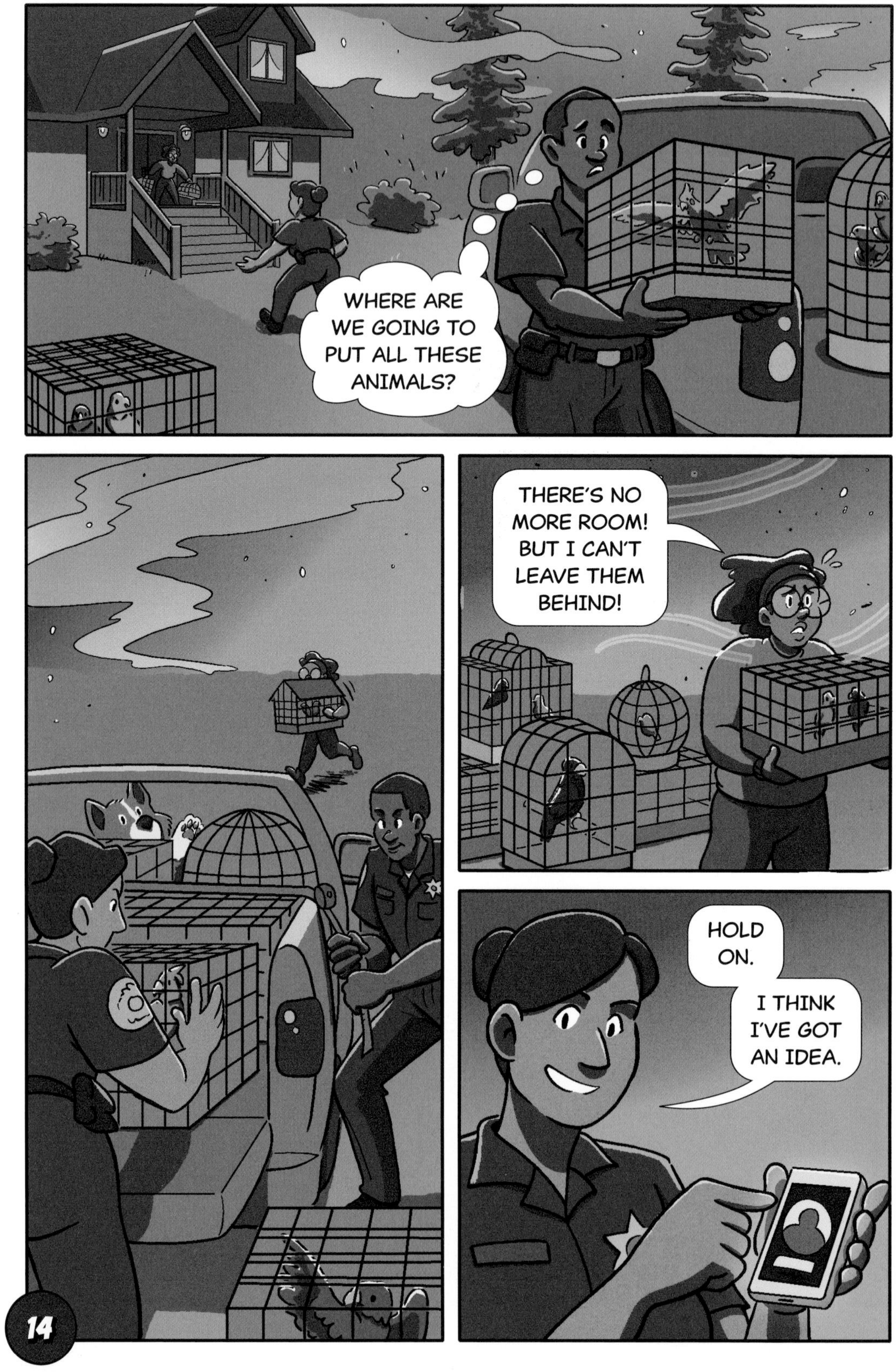
WHERE ARE WE GOING TO PUT ALL THESE ANIMALS?
THERE'S NO MORE ROOM! BUT I CAN'T LEAVE THEM BEHIND!
HOLD ON.
I THINK I'VE GOT AN IDEA.

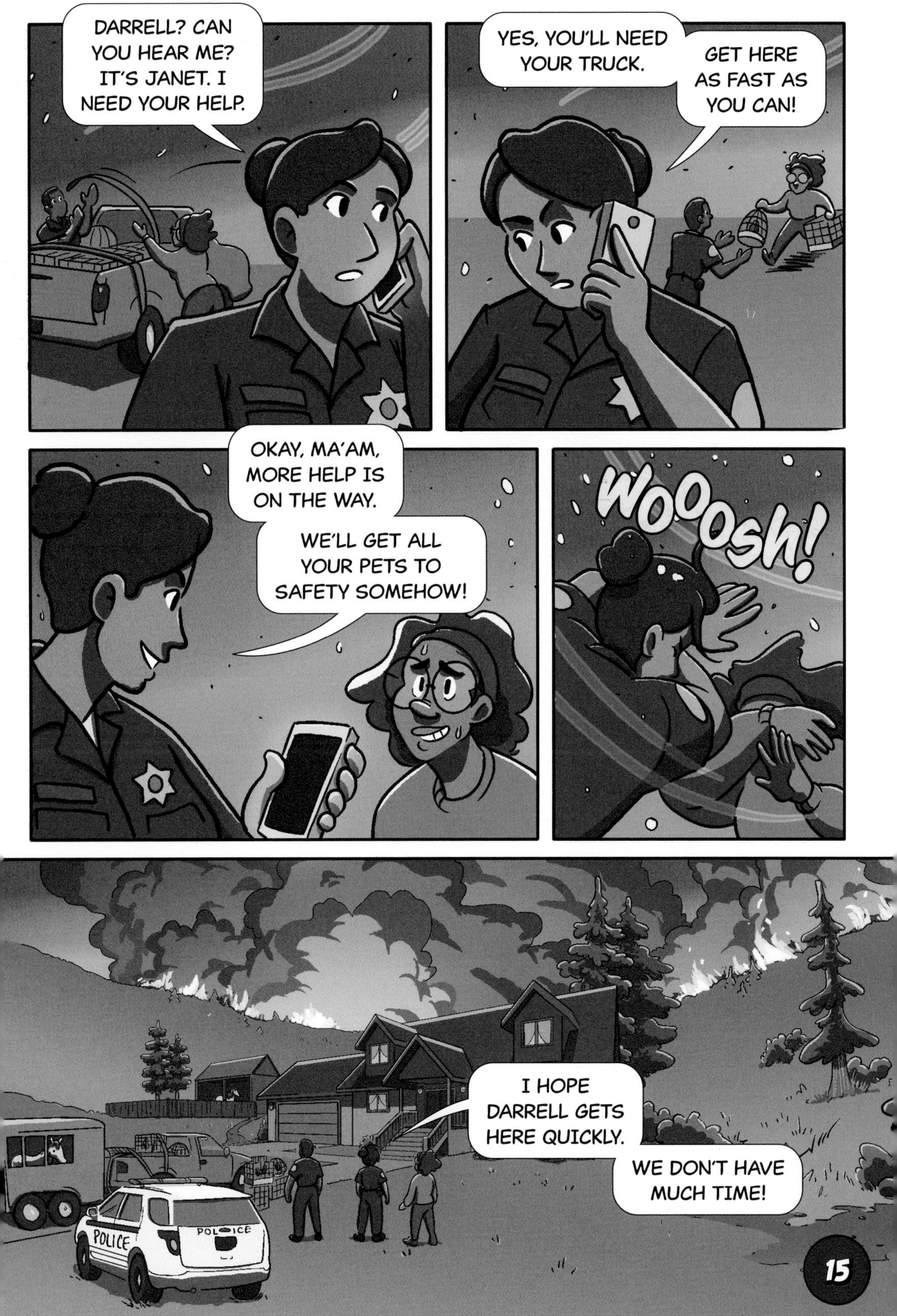
DARRELL? CAN YOU HEAR ME? IT'S JANET. I NEED YOUR HELP.
YES, YOU'LL NEED YOUR TRUCK.
GET HERE AS FAST AS YOU CAN!
OKAY, MA'AM, MORE HELP IS ON THE WAY.
WE'LL GET ALL YOUR PETS TO SAFETY SOMEHOW!
WOOOSH!
POLICE
POLICE
I HOPE DARRELL GETS HERE QUICKLY.
WE DON'T HAVE MUCH TIME!

CHAPTER 4
Bird Rescue

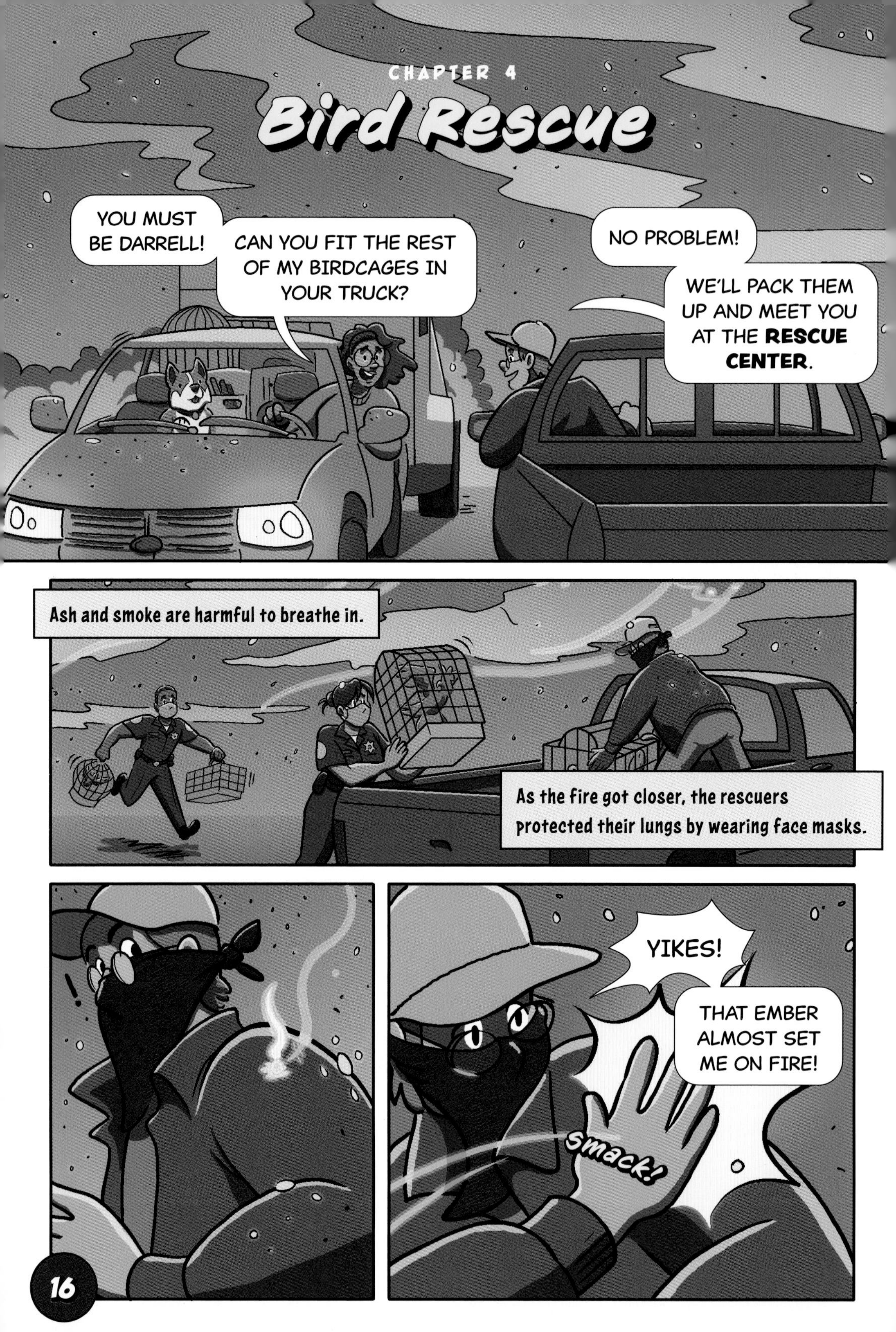

YOU MUST BE DARRELL!
CAN YOU FIT THE REST OF MY BIRDCAGES IN YOUR TRUCK?
NO PROBLEM!
WE'LL PACK THEM UP AND MEET YOU AT THE **RESCUE CENTER**.
Ash and smoke are harmful to breathe in.
As the fire got closer, the rescuers protected their lungs by wearing face masks.
!
YIKES!
THAT EMBER ALMOST SET ME ON FIRE!
Smack!

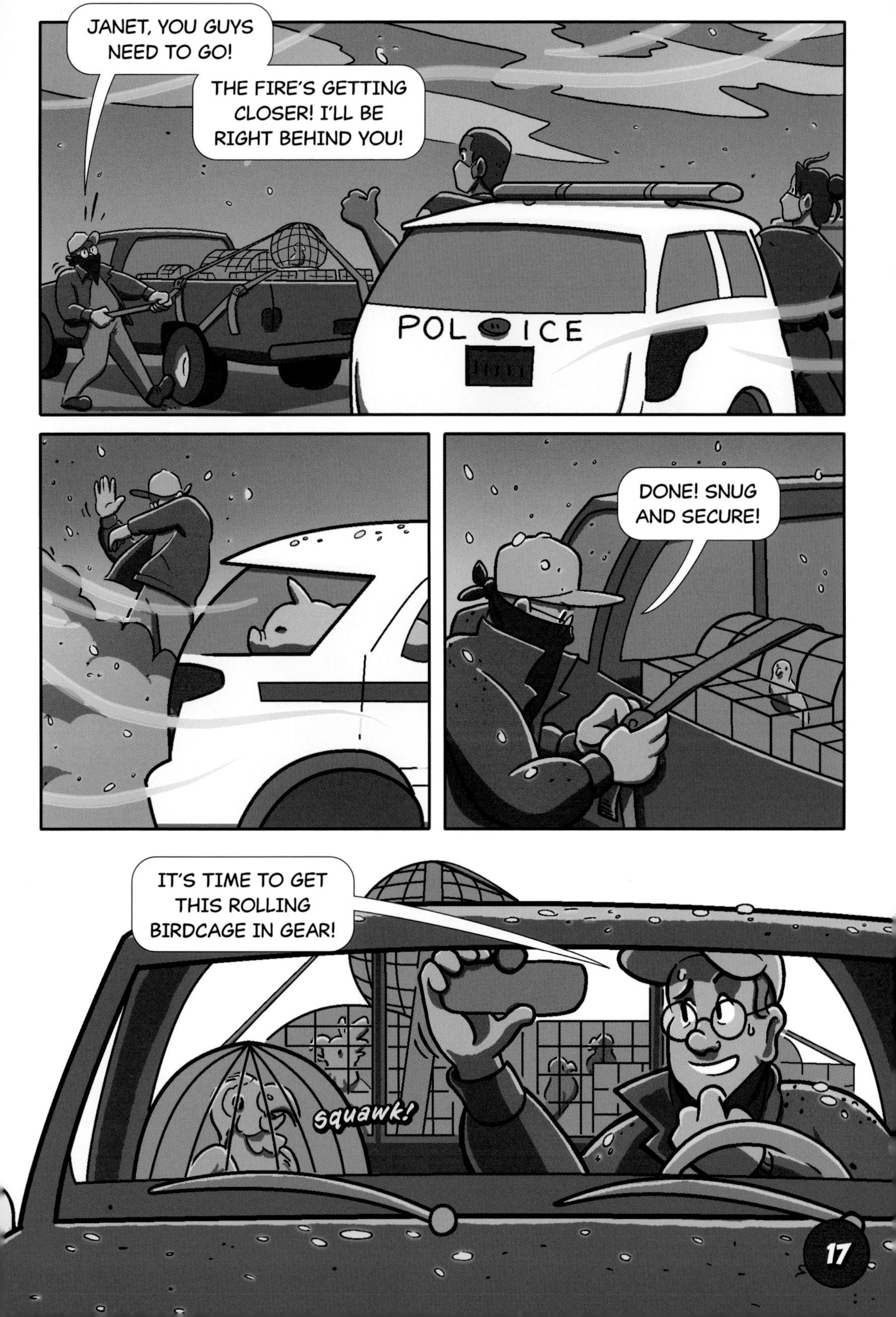
JANET, YOU GUYS NEED TO GO!
THE FIRE'S GETTING CLOSER! I'LL BE RIGHT BEHIND YOU!
POLICE
DONE! SNUG AND SECURE!
IT'S TIME TO GET THIS ROLLING BIRDCAGE IN GEAR!
squawk!

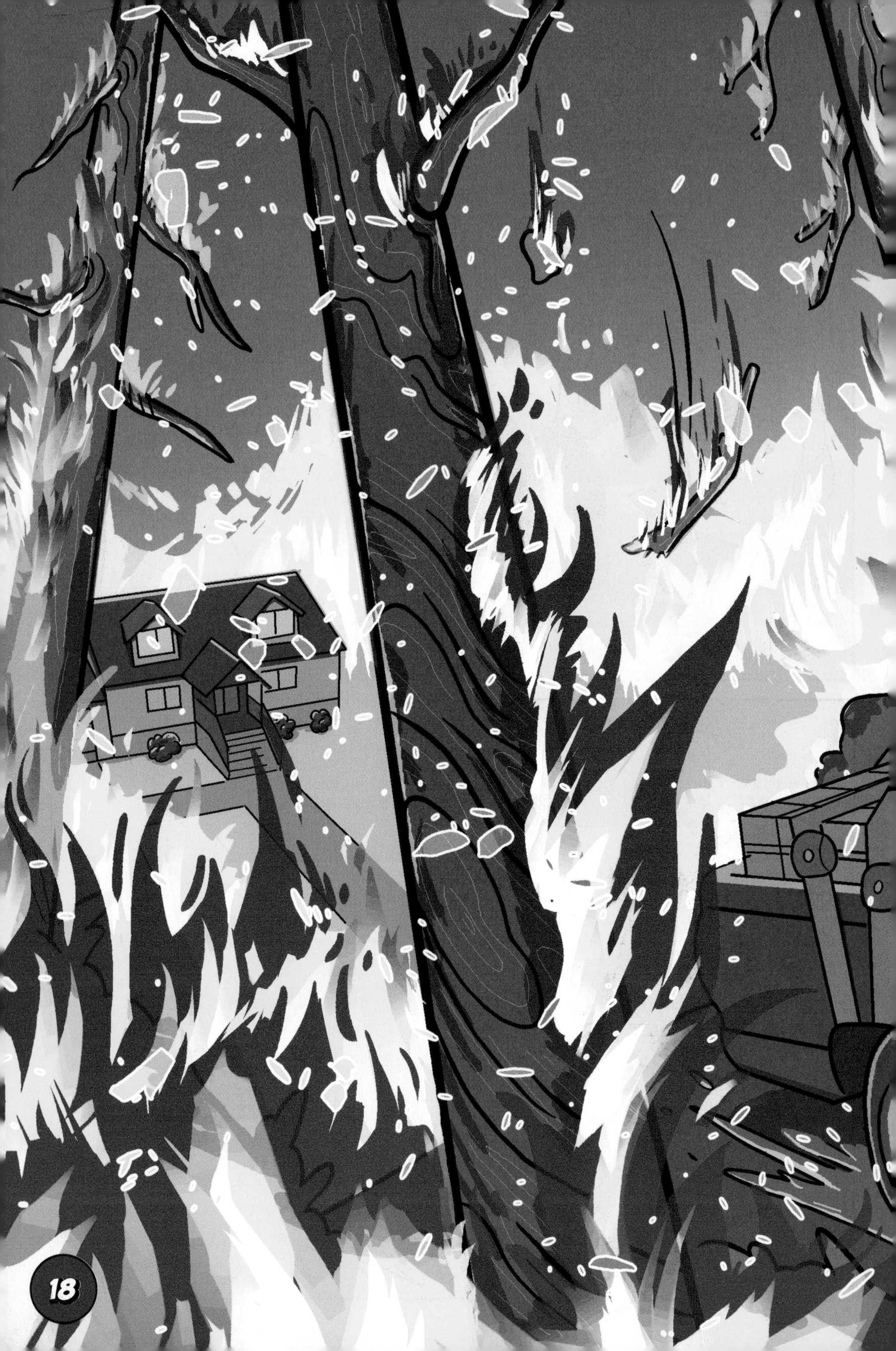

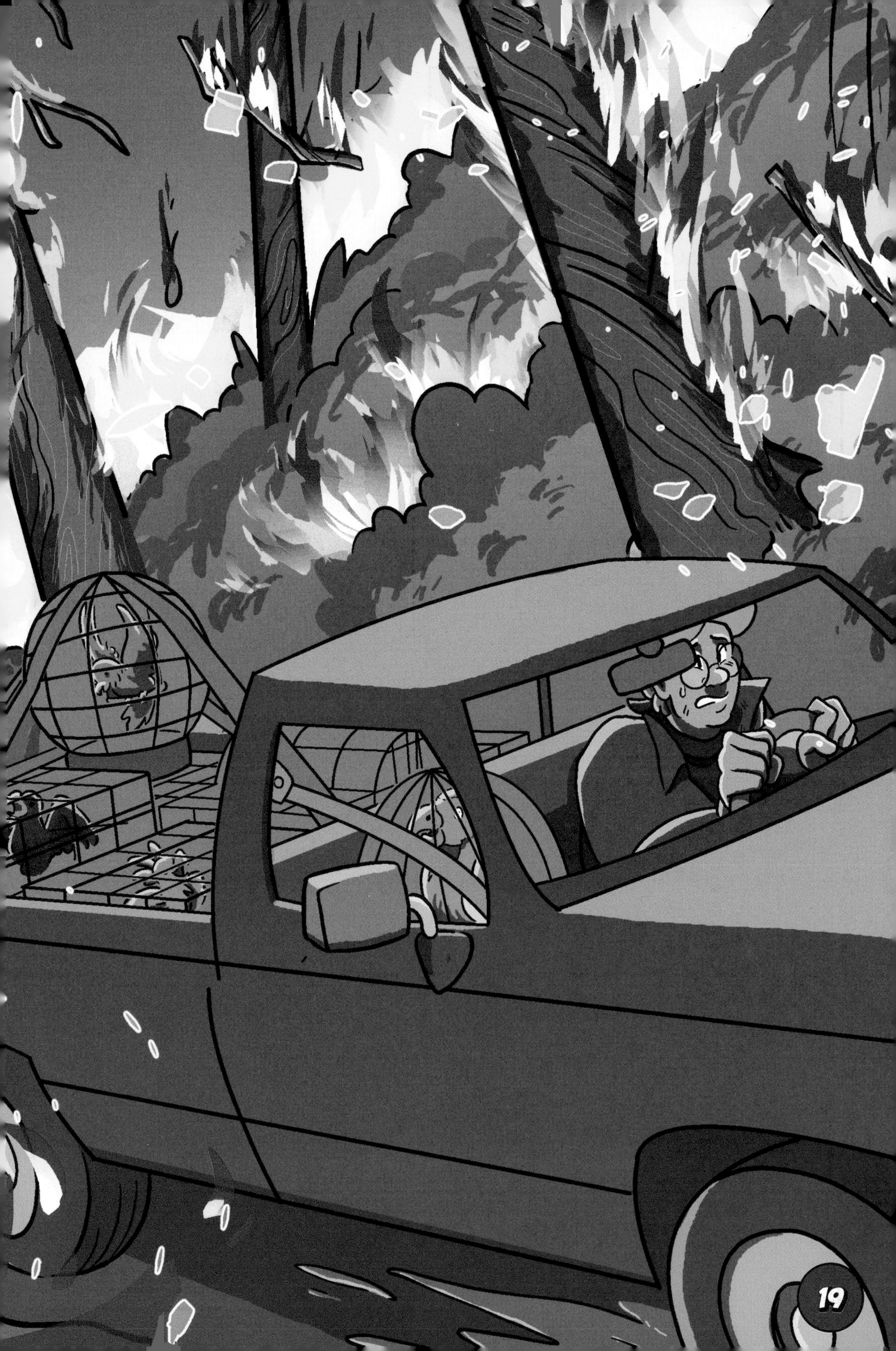

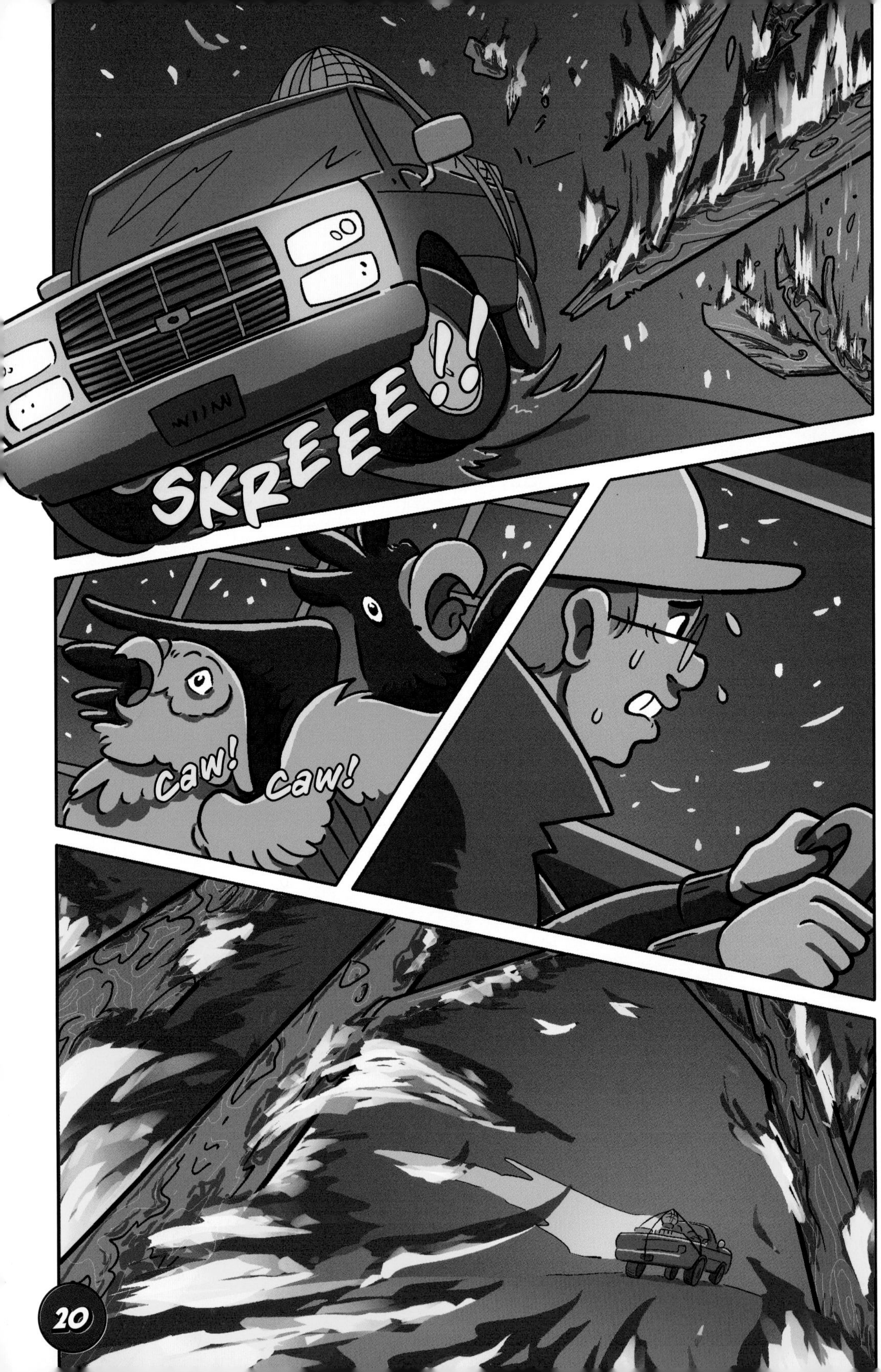
SKREEE
!!
caw!
caw!

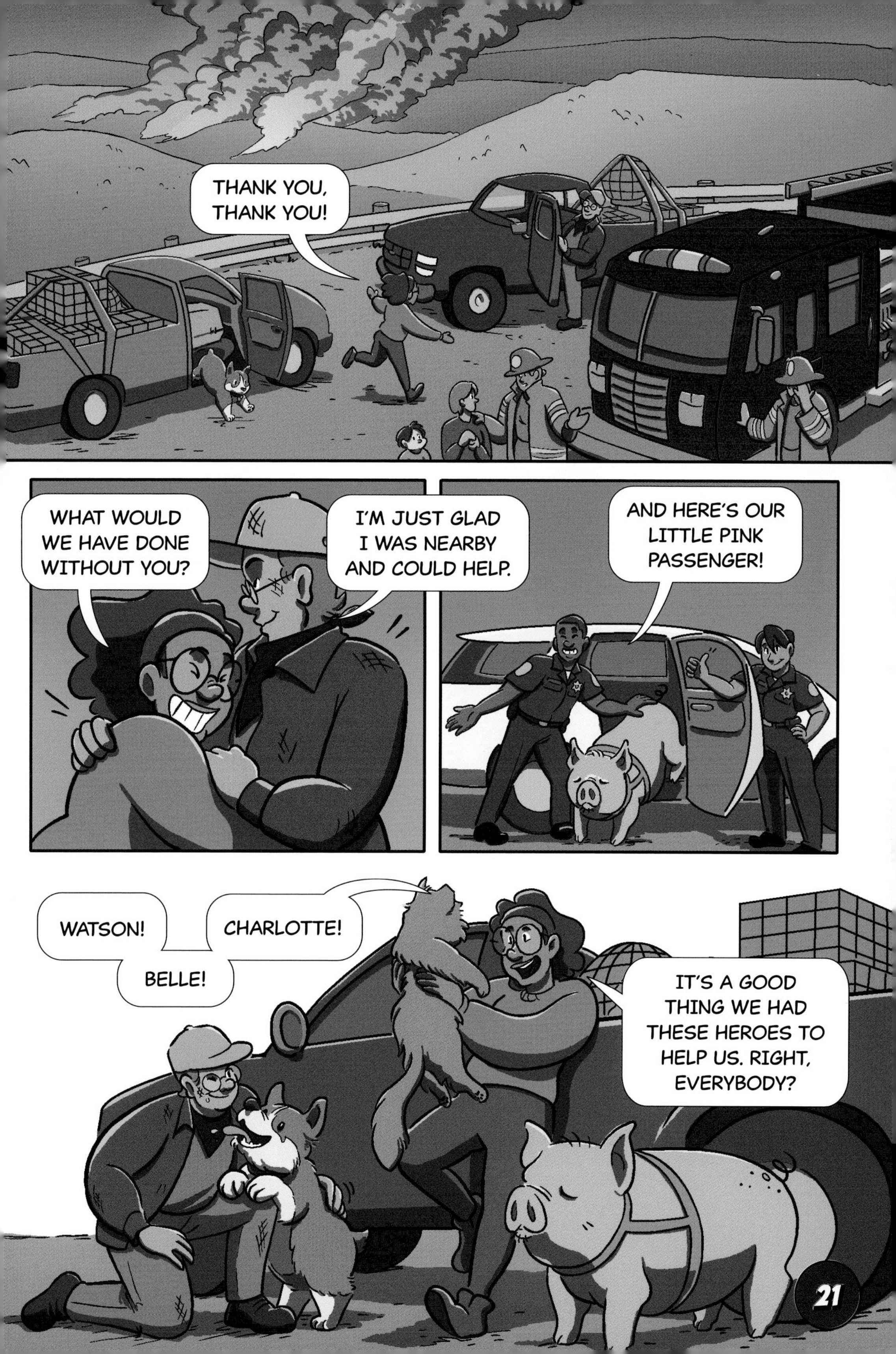
THANK YOU, THANK YOU!
WHAT WOULD WE HAVE DONE WITHOUT YOU?
I'M JUST GLAD I WAS NEARBY AND COULD HELP.
AND HERE'S OUR LITTLE PINK PASSENGER!
WATSON!
CHARLOTTE!
BELLE!
IT'S A GOOD THING WE HAD THESE HEROES TO HELP US. RIGHT, EVERYBODY?

OTHER
WILDFIRE RESCUES

THOMAS FIRE
CALIFORNIA

In December 2017, hot weather and
high winds quickly spread the flames
of the Thomas Fire. **Volunteers** raced
to rescue animals from the **rapidly**
spreading flames. They brought cats,
dogs, pigs, goats, chickens, donkeys,
and even an emu to shelters. Members of the
Southern California Emergency **Equine** Evacuation
saved more than 100 horses from ranches in the
path of the fire. Several llamas were taken to a
beach out of harm's way.

RUSSIAN WILDFIRES
RUSSIA

In parts of Russia, the summer of
2010 was the hottest in more than
100 years. Soon, forests caught fire
and hundreds of wildfires burned
at once. In early August, a wildfire
spread toward an animal shelter near the capital
city of Moscow. The shelter was home to dogs
and cats, as well as monkeys and bears that were
once used as circus animals. Flames got as close
as about 450 feet (137 m) from the shelter before
volunteers were able to put out the fire.

GLOSSARY

embers small bits of flying, burning material

enormous very, very large

equine having to do with horses

evacuate to leave from an area of danger

feed box a container for animal food

rapidly very quickly

rescue center a safe place to go during an emergency

volunteers people who work without pay

wildfires fires in woodlands

woodlands large areas of trees and other plants

INDEX

READ MORE

Rowell, Rebecca. *The World's Wildfires (Special Reports).* Minneapolis: Abdo Publishing, 2021.

Smith, Emma Bland. *Escaping the Fire (Gavin McNally's Year Off).* Minneapolis: Spellbound, 2020.

Waeschle, Amy. *Daring Wildlife Rescues (Edge Books. Rescued!).* North Mankato, MN: Capstone Press, 2018.

LEARN MORE ONLINE

1. Go to **www.factsurfer.com**
2. Enter "**Wildfire Escape**" into the search box.
3. Click on the cover of this book to see a list of websites.